Juan Ponce de Leon and the Discovery of Florida

Painting of Juan Ponce de Leon on a Spanish postage stamp (Courtesy of the State Archives of Florida)

Juan Ponce de Leon
and the Discovery of Florida

Sandra Wallus Sammons

Pineapple Press, Inc.
Sarasota, Florida

For Robert Edmund Sammons, David Robert Sammons, and Calvin Robert Sammons—three generations in a family that makes my own life a wonderful adventure

Copyright © 2013 by Sandra Wallus Sammons

Inquiries should be addressed to:

Pineapple Press, Inc.
P.O. Box 3889
Sarasota, Florida 34230

www.pineapplepress.com

ISBN 978-1-56164-592-3 (hardback)
ISBN 978-1-56164-593-0 (paperback)
ISBN 978-1-56164-615-9 (e-book)

Library of Congress Cataloging-in-Publication Data

Sammons, Sandra Wallus.
    Juan Ponce de Leon and the discovery of Florida / Sandra Wallus Sammons.
        p. cm.
    Includes bibliographical references and index.
    ISBN 978-1-56164-592-3 (hardcover : alk. paper) -- ISBN 978-1-56164-593-0 (pbk. : alk. paper)
    1. Ponce de León, Juan, 1460?-1521--Juvenile literature. 2. Explorers--America--Biography--Juvenile literature. 3. Explorers--Spain--Biography--Juvenile literature. 4. Florida--Discovery and exploration--Spanish--Juvenile literature. I. Title.
    E125.P7S28 2013
    975.9'01092--dc23
    [B]
                                          2012041609

First Edition
10 9 8 7 6 5 4 3 2 1

Design by Shé Hicks
Printed in the United States of America

"I have only told the half of what I saw."
– Marco Polo

Contents

Foreword

The first permanent colony by Europeans on Florida soil was at St. Augustine in 1565, but much led up to that settlement. More than fifty years before, another explorer from Spain set foot on a beautiful Florida beach and gave it the name "La Florida," Land of the Flowers.

That explorer was Juan Ponce de Leon, a name well known in the Caribbean islands of the Dominican Republic and Puerto Rico, as well as in Florida.

While writing this biography, I took a plane trip south from Virginia to Florida, and from the air, the eastern coastline of our Sunshine State is very clear. You can see all the rivers and inlets. Christopher Columbus and Juan Ponce de Leon did not have the ability to see the world from that point of view. Columbus and Ponce didn't even know this land was here!

In the 1400s, most people just knew about their own

little section of the world. For years people even thought the world was flat. If you sailed too far, they said, you would fall off the edge. By the end of the 1400s, however, most educated people knew that the earth was round. They just did not know the exact shape of the ball, or how large or small it was.

The European countries just 500 years ago did not look the same as they do today, either. In this biography, we call Ponce's country "Spain," but it was, at that time, two small kingdoms that had united, with a king of Aragon and a queen of Castile. Later, more kingdoms would come together to create the Spain we know now. There was trade with other countries, but trade routes, by land or sea, were very dangerous.

There were no books as we know them today until the printing press was invented sometime around 1450. Then many people in Spain read about Marco Polo's fantastic trip to China in 1271 with his father and uncle. Many people started dreaming of traveling to far-off, exotic lands.

Dreaming changed to reality after 1492. Soon after the first look at land in what we now call the Americas, explorers would travel around the entire globe.

Let us look at Juan Ponce de Leon's world.

Chapter 1

Young Juan Ponce de Leon

Juan Ponce de Leon lived over 500 years ago, in what we now call the fifteenth century. He was probably born in 1474. We have to guess at some things about his life, because few records are available from that time.

We do know that he was born in what we now call Spain, in the province of Valladolid. His parents were probably influential people in Spanish society, and Juan was educated by a relative, Don Pedro Nunez de Guzman. Guzman was known for his skill at teaching young men the art of warfare. When he was older, Juan joined the many other young men who were defending their country.

Spain in those days was struggling with people who

had invaded their land many years before. The Moors ruled the country and spread their own Muslim religion. The Spaniards wanted to rule themselves and to practice their own Catholic religion. For many years, young Spanish men became soldiers, fighting to defeat the Moors and send them out of their land.

Juan Ponce de Leon had been trained well and became a good soldier. The Moors were determined fighters, but finally, when Ponce was almost twenty years old, the war was over. In 1492 in the province of Granada, the Moors finally stopped fighting, and hundreds of years of warfare came to an end. Spain was once again free to have its own religion and its own government.

With no wars to fight, many young, brave Spanish soldiers were out of work. The Spanish government needed gold to fill up its treasury. It was time to look for new places to sell items made by Spaniards. Trade would bring in money and create jobs for the people.

Since ancient times there had been trade with countries in the Far East, sometimes called the East Indies. The Europeans knew that if they traveled east by land, they would reach China, Japan, and India. There they could trade their goods for silks and spices and other exotic items. However, between Europe and the East Indies were dangerously high mountains and miles of

Spanish flag (Courtesy of the State Archives of Florida)

deserts. There were also raiders, lying in wait for traders taking that route.

Mapmakers told them the earth was round. Could there possibly be another route to this wonderful land of the East Indies—by sea?

A sailor from Portugal, Bartholemew Diaz, sailed south along the west coast of Africa until in 1488 he reached the continent's southern tip, the Cape of Good Hope. From there, he would have to sail east to the East Indies. Winds and tides were treacherous, but at least one sea route was possible.

A sailor from Italy, Christopher Columbus, wanted to try a different way. Columbus had been studying maps created by another Italian, Paolo dal Pozzo Toscanelli. They showed the East Indies on the other side of the ocean that started on Europe's west coast. The maps helped convince Columbus that these lands could be reached by sailing west. If the earth was round, then why not take the opposite route around the ball? An interesting idea, but he couldn't find anyone to finance his trip.

After failing to convince the governments of other countries of his idea, this Italian sailor happened to be in Spain when the Moors were defeated in Granada. The long war was over. King Ferdinand and Queen Isabella were interested in helping Columbus try out his idea.

Chapter 2

Christopher Columbus Finds a New World

On August 3, 1492, a very excited forty-year-old Christopher Columbus sailed west. On his three ships, the *Nina*, the *Pinta,* and the *Santa Maria,* were about 200 men and supplies for a long voyage. The trouble was, Columbus did not know how long the voyage would be.

There had probably been others who ventured out into this "Ocean Sea" (the Atlantic Ocean) before 1492, but Columbus had no records of their journeys. The *Nina*, the *Pinta,* and the *Santa Maria* were sailing into unknown waters. According to the maps Columbus had studied, Japan and China were on the other side. But he didn't know that for sure. He hoped the maps were not mistaken.

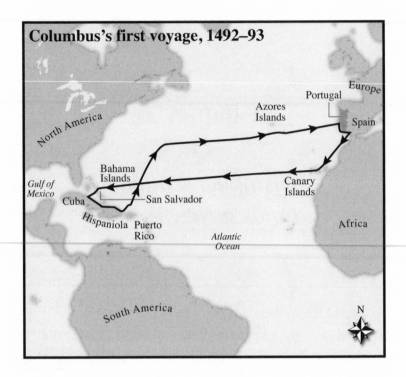

Columbus's first voyage, 1492–93

Trade winds helped to push the ships across the miles and miles of ocean, but after weeks of not seeing land, the men became discouraged. They urged Columbus to turn back, to return to Spain. Suddenly land was sighted in the distance!

Columbus was right. If you sailed far enough across the ocean, you would come to land. And Columbus hoped that Toscanelli's map was correct. Surely they had reached the East Indies.

They landed on October 12, 1492. They looked around them. The sun lit up the cobalt blue and emerald

A drawing of Christopher Columbus, his men, and the natives on Hispaniola, 1492 (Courtesy of the State Archives of Florida)

green colors in the water. There was an amazing variety of palms and lush plants covering the land. It was different from home, but, thought Columbus, was it Japan, China, or India?

Whatever it was, they felt they should claim the land for Spain. As the men placed the flag of Spain in the sand, eyes were watching from the bushes. The natives, who had lived there for thousands of years, were cautious because neighboring tribes would sometimes come to attack their villages. They looked over the newcomers carefully.

Columbus and his men seemed to be friendly, and they were certainly different from anyone else who had landed on their island. The natives thought they must have come from the sky! When the strangers offered gifts, the natives welcomed them.

While the natives looked over the strangers, Columbus was also trying to figure out the natives. They didn't look like the Chinese whom Marco Polo had described. But still hopeful that he had really reached the East Indies, Columbus noted in his log book that he had met the natives, and they were "Indians."

The natives loved the glass beads and other trinkets the visitors had brought. They also gave gifts. Beautifully colored live parrots were presented to the Spaniards. The

Indians then allowed the men to look over their island. Columbus named the beautiful island San Salvador, in honor of the Savior of their Catholic faith.

There were many natives on this island and on other islands nearby. They grew their own vegetables and ate fish from the ocean. They made their own pottery and had their own religion and culture.

The Spaniards stayed a short time on San Salvador and then sailed to other islands. Again the Indians were friendly. On one island, which Columbus named Hispaniola, his flagship ran aground on a sand bar. Unable to fix the *Santa Maria*, Columbus had to leave it, along with about forty men, on that island. He told them to start a new settlement, which he named Villa de la Navidad, or Town of the Nativity.

After making such tremendous discoveries about what was across the Ocean Sea, Columbus was anxious to return to Spain to tell the king and queen about his adventure. Leaving food and supplies for the men who would stay at La Navidad, Columbus assured them that he would return soon with more settlers and supplies. Taking some of the parrots, a small amount of gold, and other gifts from the natives, Columbus found his way back to Spain.

There was much excitement when Columbus met

with the king and queen, and he gladly answered their many questions. They had traveled uncharted seas and found unknown lands. They had made the voyage and returned after more than 200 days to tell about it! It was an amazing accomplishment.

King Ferdinand and Queen Isabella realized their money had been well spent on what had seemed a crazy idea. No one, not even Columbus, was sure if he had reached the East Indies, but right now they concentrated on what he had found!

For his bravery, the royal couple gave Christopher Columbus the title of Viceroy and Admiral of the Ocean Sea. He would also be called Don (or Sir) Christopher Columbus. And his eldest son would inherit those titles after his death.

The word spread throughout Europe, and young Spanish soldiers who no longer had to fight the Moors were listening. They, too, then dreamed of exploring this unknown world. Perhaps they, too, could find adventure, and perhaps riches, beyond the Ocean Sea.

One of those young soldiers was Juan Ponce de Leon.

Chapter 3

A New World for Ponce de Leon

On his second voyage at the end of September of 1493, Columbus had no trouble enlisting more than 1,000 men to travel with him in seventeen ships. His flagship, or lead ship, was named the *Santa Maria la Galante* (Saint Mary the Gallant), after his trusted ship on the first voyage. On board there were sailors, soldiers, and skilled workmen to help create new settlements on the many islands Columbus would now claim for Spain. Priests came to teach the Catholic faith to the natives. On board were also 200 "gentlemen volunteers," one of whom was probably Juan Ponce de Leon.

The trip took just over twenty days, and this time they knew what to expect when they reached land. By

November of 1493 the fleet reached the Caribbean Sea. They stopped at several new ports on this trip, including an island the natives called Boriquen, which we now know as Puerto Rico. But Columbus did not stay long. He was anxious to get back to Hispaniola to check on the men he had left behind.

Unfortunately, the new settlement, La Navidad, was no more. The town had burned to the ground, and there were no Spaniards left alive.

Horrified at what had happened, Columbus was still determined to make a permanent settlement. He had come all the way across the Ocean Sea to do just that. The ships sailed farther along the coast and found another fine harbor. Columbus would name his new settlement La Isabella, after the Spanish queen.

But again they had problems. Columbus was a good sailor, but he was not a good administrator of a colony. The men started building a fortress, and since they had claimed the land for Spain, they expected the natives to work for them. The natives were no longer friendly. Busy building the town, the Spaniards had not taken the time to learn about the foods there. Their food supply ran low.

Columbus sent some of his ships back to Spain for more food and supplies. On hearing that the settlement was in trouble, the king and queen sent other administrators to replace Columbus. One of those administrators was Nicolas de Ovando.

Nicolas de Ovando arrived with thirty-two ships and over 2,000 men and women. Ovando was to be governor of the island, with instructions from the king and queen to bring order to the growing colony. That he was determined to do.

The natives on Hispaniola were called Tainos, part of a group of natives who spoke the Arawak language. They had lived undisturbed for many years, except for some invasions by the Caribs, natives of other islands.

A group of Tainos Indians row out to greet a Spanish ship in their dugout canoe. Courtesy of Hector A. Garcia, Salon Hogar

Friendly at first to the strangers, they soon resented the Spaniards taking their land, forcing them to work, and trying to teach them a new religion.

An old Spanish cathedral, a Catholic church. This one is in St. Augustine. (Courtesy of the State Archives of Florida)

The Spaniards firmly believed that their God required them to spread their Catholic faith, and that they had a right to claim this New World as their own. The Tainos waited. By 1504, the Tainos rebelled.

The natives made their stand against the Spaniards on the eastern side of the island, in a province called Higuey. The Tainos had spears made of wood and bows with arrows. The Spaniards had metal weapons, crossbows, and an early type of gun. The Tainos didn't have a chance. Being an experienced soldier, Juan Ponce de Leon had a major role in the fighting.

One of the hats worn by the Spanish soldiers. (Courtesy of June Cussen)

With the Tainos defeated, the Spanish continued their settlement. Governor Ovando, however, must have noticed Ponce de Leon's bravery in battle and wanted to show his appreciation. He appointed Ponce to be the frontier governor of the province in which the battle was fought, Higuey. Ponce was given a large land grant, perhaps about 200 acres, so he could start a farm. He was also given some Taino Indians to work for him.

Juan Ponce de Leon worked with the Tainos and became a successful farmer. The natives taught him that the yucca plant grew well in the sandy soil, and that the roots of the yucca plant could be made into cassava bread.

Because his farm was located on the eastern end of the island, he was close to the town of Boca de Yuma (Bay of Yuma), the port from which ships left for their month-long trip back to Spain. Ship captains heading across the Ocean Sea stopped there to buy supplies. They bought many loaves of cassava bread, because it was found to stay fresh during the trip to Europe.

Juan Ponce de Leon was happy, successful, and getting wealthy as a farmer. But perhaps there were more lands to explore.

Chapter 4

Governor of a Province

By 1505, Frontier Governor Ponce de Leon was asked by Governor Ovando to build a new Spanish settlement in the province of Higuey on the island of Hispaniola. Ponce named the new town Salvaleon.

Governor Ponce also started his own family. He chose Leonor, the Spanish-born daughter of an innkeeper, to be his wife. They soon had four children. Juana, Isabel, and Maria were his daughters, and Luis was his son. For his growing family, he built a large house made of stone.

Ponce was a well-respected governor and successful farmer. He had friends among the natives as well as the ship captains coming into Hispaniola's ports. Ponce heard stories told by natives visiting from other

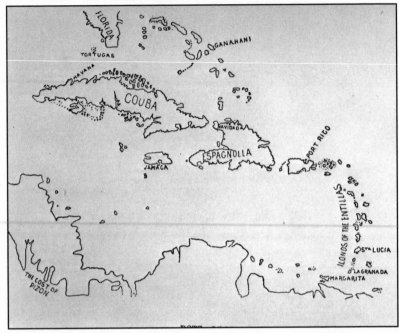

Map showing Cuba, Hispaniola, Puerto Rico, and Florida (Courtesy of the State Archives of Florida)

islands. Hispaniola is one of a long chain of islands in the Caribbean Sea, and Ponce could almost see the next island to the east from Salvaleon. Columbus had stopped there briefly on his second voyage, and Ponce had seen it at that time. The native name for it was Boriquen, but now we call it Puerto Rico.

The Tainos who lived on Puerto Rico told stories of their bountiful land, with fertile soil and with gold in the rivers. Ponce, the successful farmer, was still interested in finding gold. The desire to explore the next island was too much to resist.

In the days of the early explorers to the New World, European governments divided up the area. Sailors from each country could only visit lands to which their government had claimed rights. The Spanish king and queen, for example, were not supposed to have their explorers visit lands that had already been claimed by Portugal. And an explorer also could not claim rights to a place already claimed by someone from his own country. Ponce learned that a Spaniard named Vicente Yanez Pinzon had been asked to make a settlement on Puerto Rico. However, Pinzon had not yet completed his assignment.

Historians know that Ponce made an "official" trip to Puerto Rico in 1508, but there is evidence that he made a trip quietly before that. Two years earlier, he landed some ships at El Aguada, the "watering hole," on the western side of the island. He knew that port because Columbus had stopped there, with Ponce on board, about fifteen years before. Many Spanish ships made this a regular stop on their journeys. It was known for its good fresh water and sailors could fill their water casks before going off to explore other islands.

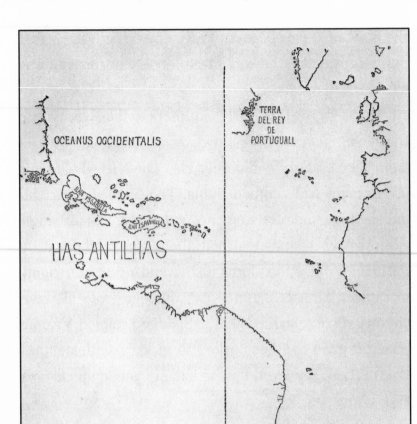

Map showing Portugal's territory (Courtesy of the State Archives of Florida)

He knew there was fresh water, but would he find gold?

Speaking with the local Tainos, Ponce learned that there might be a better port on the other side of the island. Some of the crew hiked across the island to find it. They took soundings of the water on that side to make sure it was deep enough for their ships. They hiked back to tell the others. Not only had they found a harbor, but they had found gold in the streams!

Excited by both finds, Ponce sent some of his crew sailing around the island to the new port. Ponce himself and some of the men hiked across, making maps of the island as they walked along. One legend has it that when he saw it, Ponce exclaimed: "Que puerto tan rico!" ("What a rich harbor!") This port would later be called San Juan Bay and the whole island would later be called Puerto Rico.

Before leaving, Ponce realized that a hill nearby would make the ideal spot for a new capital for the island. The men started building some homes made of cane and thatch. Ponce named the new settlement Caparra.

Chapter 5

Governor of an Island

By 1508 King Ferdinand gave his permission for Juan Ponce de Leon to explore Puerto Rico. Pinzon's time had run out so it was time for someone else to make a permanent settlement.

That summer, Ponce de Leon made another trip from Hispaniola with about fifty men in one ship. They built more homes and a fort, which became the primary Spanish settlement in Puerto Rico. Ponce built a sturdy home for his family and started a large garden.

Ponce had the men work on two things: planting food and finding gold. They planted yucca and built an oven for baking cassava bread. They planted a few crops for their own survival, but much of their time and energy was spent searching for gold.

King Ferdinand named Ponce de Leon governor of the new island on August 14, 1509. Now Juan Ponce de Leon was both frontier governor of Higuey province on Hispaniola, and also governor of the settlement at Puerto Rico. He was asked to further settle the island and to continue looking for gold.

Juan Ponce de Leon brought his wife and children to Puerto Rico. This beautiful tropical island would be their new home.

The Taino Indians on Puerto Rico, however, had different ideas. The Spanish were spreading their settlements all over their land. And the Tainos were supposed to work for them. Again, what had started out as a friendly sharing of the land went wrong. They did not understand why they should give up the land they had lived on for many years and be forced to work for the Spaniards.

Ponce de Leon kept peace as much as possible. Many other new settlers working with the natives, however, treated them badly. If the Indians refused to work, they received cruel punishment.

Life for the Tainos was hard, and it was even worse when disease began to spread. People living on an island have a resistance to germs that their bodies have grown used to. When new people arrive on the island, they can bring diseases to which the natives have no resistance.

The Tainos worked in the fields or gathered small chunks of gold, but many became very sick and died from diseases brought by the Spaniards. Measles and chickenpox were unknown to the natives, and they had no ability to fight those germs.

For a short time the natives worked for the Spaniards. But there were constant rebellions. However, the natives' spears and bows were no match for the Spanish metal weapons.

Chapter 6

Discovering Florida

The Tainos were not the only ones unhappy with a Spanish settlement on Puerto Rico.

When Christopher Columbus completed his first voyage to the New World, he was given many rewards. He was named Viceroy and Admiral of the Ocean Sea by the Spanish king and queen in 1493. He was told that he would govern any and all islands he would discover. And he was promised that when he died, his son would have all those titles and rights as well.

When Columbus died in 1506, his eldest son, Diego, tried to claim the titles and rights that belonged to him. The king and queen, however, had already placed Nicolas Ovando as governor of Hispaniola, and Juan Ponce de

Leon as governor of Puerto Rico, two islands Columbus had discovered. Diego did not agree with the king's appointments on those islands. His father had discovered them. Diego felt he had the legal right to govern them. Diego Columbus went to court.

The king and queen now regretted giving so many honors to Columbus, but they were forced to admit that Diego was right. Diego became the Second Admiral of the Ocean Sea, and would be called Viceroy of Hispaniola. On July 10, 1509, Diego Columbus, the son and heir of Christopher Columbus, arrived in Hispaniola. Governor Nicolas Ovando left the island.

Although they gave Diego rights to Hispaniola, the king and queen told him to allow Ponce de Leon to govern Puerto Rico. Diego, however, wanted his full share. He did whatever he could to make it hard for Ponce to govern that island.

Ponce appealed to the king and queen, but he could not fight Diego's determination to control both islands. Ponce had been loyal to the king and queen and lived as peaceably as possible with the natives. He was a respected administrator. But it was clear now that he could no longer remain at his job.

If Ponce de Leon had been able to remain governor

of Puerto Rico, he may not have discovered Florida. And since Ponce de Leon named Florida, who knows what name our state might have had?

By 1511, there were many explorers in the New World. They were claiming lands for Spain or other countries. There were rumors of other islands, farther to the northwest, yet to be explored. They had not been discovered by Christopher Columbus, so Diego could make no claim on them. And if they were to be claimed for Spain, a Spaniard would have to find them quickly before an explorer from another country could.

To take Ponce out of a bad situation and also to reward him for his continued loyalty, the king and queen gave him the rights to sail to the lands to the northwest and claim them for Spain. Ponce, not quite forty years old, readily agreed to the new venture.

In February of 1512 a royal contract was sent to him to find and make settlement on islands thought to be to the north of those already discovered. Mapmakers thought there was a large island or group of islands called Bimini in that area. Ponce would be named governor for life of any lands he discovered. He would also share in the wealth if gold were found there.

Ponce was enthusiastic about the new opportunity.

Although he had been comfortable on Puerto Rico, this was a chance to get away from Diego Columbus and also to explore a totally new area.

He equipped three ships, the *Santiago*, the *San Cristobal,* and the *Santa Maria de la Consolacion*. Both sailors and soldiers made up his crew of 65 men. Most of the food on board probably came from his farm in Salvaleon.

He set out from Puerto Rico on March 3, 1513, sailing northwest along the great chain of the Lucayos, which we now call the Bahama Islands. They continued on their course for the next several days, across open water. On March 27, Easter Sunday, they sighted land.

They approached the coast on April 2 and landed on April 3, 1513. Since they had seen only islands in their travels, Ponce believed this to be another island. It was the Easter season, Pascua Florida, or Festival of the Flowers, so he named it La Florida.

The exact location of their landing is still not known. They may have reached as far north as where St. Augustine is today. Other historians are sure that his ships couldn't have traveled that far without seeing land, and think he stopped at what is now called Ponce Inlet, just north of New Smyrna Beach. Others think his landing was farther yet to the south, near today's Melbourne Beach.

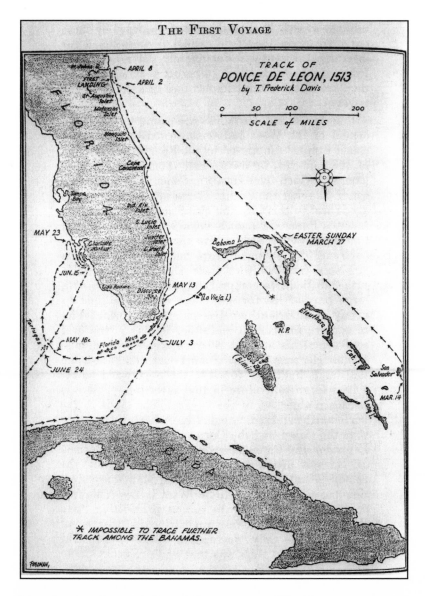

Map showing Ponce de Leon's first voyage to Florida. (Courtesy of the State Archives of Florida)

We do know that the ships landed along the east coast of today's Florida, and they took possession of the land for Spain, and named it. After five days, they left there, possibly sailing north for a short distance before turning south again. They wanted to know more about this new "island."

As they continued south, they encountered another surprise. Their ships sailed into a current that was so strong that it pushed them backwards. Instead of sailing south as they intended, the current pushed them to the northeast. They had to quickly find safe harbor. The smallest ship, the *San Cristobal*, didn't make it to safety right away. It was carried out of sight and lost for two days.

They had sailed into what we now call the Gulf Stream. The Gulf Stream is like a fast-moving river in the midst of the ocean waters. The swift current moves from the Gulf of Mexico, around Florida toward the northern United States, and then on toward Europe. Between southern Florida and the Bahama Islands, the Gulf Stream is very strong.

Ponce de Leon and his ships had just made the second great discovery of his voyage.

Chapter 7

The Other Side of the "Island"

They hugged the coast, hoping to avoid the strong current that wanted to push them backwards. They went ashore to fill their water casks several times, perhaps at places that we now call the St. Lucie River, Jupiter Inlet, Key Biscayne, and Biscayne Bay.

By the middle of May, they were sailing along the southern side of the Florida Keys. Of course, Ponce had to name them, so he called them "Los Martires" (the Martyrs). From a distance, he thought they looked like men who were suffering. The water around the keys was so shallow due to coral reefs that the ships dared not pass through until they had reached Key West. Then they finally could turn northward again to see the other side

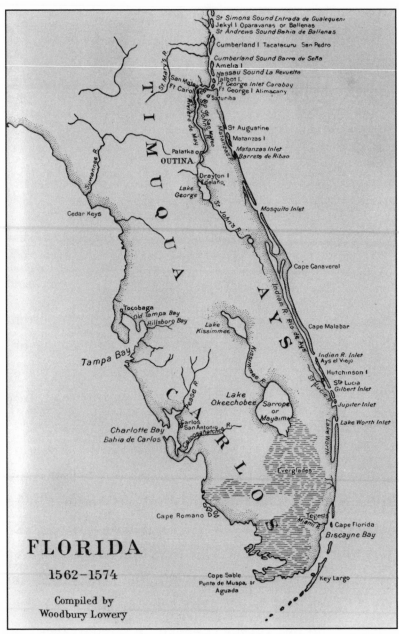

St Simons Sound Entrada de Gualequeni
Jekyl I Oparavanas or Ballenas
St Andrews Sound Bahia de Ballanas
Cumberland I Tacatacuru San Pedro
Cumberland Sound Barra de Seña
Amelia I
Nassau Sound La Revuelta
Talbot I.
Ft George Inlet Caraboy
Ft George I Alimacany
Saturiba

Rivière de May
Riv de São João
San Mateo
Ft Caroline

St Augustine
Matanzas I
Matanzas Inlet
Barrera de Ribao

St John's R.

TIMUQUA

Palatka or
OUTINA

Drayton I
Edelano

Lake
George

Suwannee R.

Cedar Keys

Mosquito Inlet

Cape Canaveral

AYS

Indian R. Rio de Ays

Tocobaga
Old Tampa Bay
Hillsboro Bay

Lake
Kissimmee

Cape Malabar

Tampa Bay

Kissimmee R.

Indian R. Inlet
Ays el Viejo
Hutchinson I

St⁴ Lucia
Gilbert Inlet

St Lucie R.

Jupiter Inlet

CARLO

Lake
Okeechobee

Sarrope
or
Mayaimi

Lake Worth Inlet

Lake Worth

Peese R.

Charlotte Bay
Bahia de Carlos

Carlos
San Antonio
Caloosahatchee R.

Everglades

Cape Romano

Tegesta
Cape Florida
Biscayne Bay

Miami R.

Cape Sable
Punta de Muspa, or
Aguada

Key Largo

FLORIDA

1562–1574

Compiled by
Woodbury Lowery

Florida and its many rivers and inlets. "Carlos" indicates where the Calusas lived. (Courtesy of the State Archives of Florida)

of the large "island" they had named La Florida.

Sailing north by northeast, they spied the mainland again on May 23rd. Again, historians dispute the location of Ponce's landing. The landing might have been at Tampa Bay, or at Charlotte Harbor, or perhaps even farther south at Cape Romano or Cape Sable, near the Florida Everglades.

Ponce still thought that La Florida was an island. Finding a good harbor, the ships anchored, took on fresh drinking water and wood for their stoves, and stayed for several days. The natives, of the Calusa tribe, seemed to be friendly at first, but soon fierce fighting broke out. Even with superior weapons, the Spaniards had to sail away to escape their attackers.

The Spaniards had heard about a small chain of islands at the west end of the Florida Keys so they made another stop. The islands were loaded with wildlife, and in one day the Spaniards caught many giant sea turtles,

⚜ The Calusa Indians were known to be fierce warriors, controlling southwest Florida at the time of Ponce's arrival. They were excellent fishermen, woodcarvers, and builders.

View of the Dry Tortugas, just west of the Florida Keys (Courtesy of the State Archives of Florida)

Caribbean monk seals, and thousands of sea birds. Ponce called the islands Las Tortugas, or "the Turtles." We now call them the Dry Tortugas. They are a short distance from Key West.

The trip had taken almost eight months, but they had discovered Florida and the Gulf Stream. They were glad to return to Puerto Rico, but were horrified by what they found there.

Caparra had been burned to the ground by the Caribs. Viceroy Diego Columbus was having trouble controlling the Taino Indians, and he was still trying to take over Ponce's authority on the island.

Ponce first made sure his family was safe. Then, knowing he would have to report to the king and queen on the islands he had found on his last voyage, he set sail for Spain. In April 1514, he was warmly received as he displayed some gold that was found and as he described the lands to the north of the already-known islands.

Like Columbus, Ponce now received many honors. He, too, would be called "Don" (or "Sir") Juan Ponce de Leon. And he would be the first Spanish explorer to be presented his own personal coat of arms.

Ponce, like Columbus and other explorers, had his discoveries drawn on the Padron Real, a large map kept in Seville, Spain. The years 1492 to 1514 were exciting years for explorers! They were changing everyone's ideas as to what the world looked like.

In September of 1514, the king signed documents appointing Juan Ponce de Leon as "Governor and Chief Justice of Bimini and Florida." Today there are islands called Bimini, in the Bahamas off the shore of Florida.

The king and queen also gave Ponce permission to make another voyage so he could make a permanent settlement on La Florida. He was given all the rules and regulations for doing so. There was one problem, though.

While Ponce was in Spain, the king and queen learned that the Caribs were attacking Puerto Rico again.

⊛ A personal coat of arms was a special design given to a person who had done something very special. It was given to honor one man, but it brought honor to his whole family for years to come.

King Ferdinand and Queen Isabella requested that Ponce defeat the warring Caribs in Puerto Rico and on other nearby islands before building a settlement in La Florida. Colonists would then be safer to live in their settlements in the New World. In addition to his other honors, he was appointed captain of a small fleet to subdue the Caribs.

This would be a real challenge.

Chapter 8

Shot by an Arrow

Juan Ponce de Leon purchased three new ships, the *Barbola*, the *Santa Maria*, and the *Santiago,* and filled them with food and weapons.

Ponce's ships left Spain on May 14, 1515, with sailors, soldiers, and colonists on board. He took what was now the usual route across the Atlantic, sailing south to the Canary Islands off the coast of Africa, and then riding the trade winds west to the newly discovered islands.

Just twenty years before, they would not have met any other ships on this route. Now there were other ships confidently coming and going across the huge ocean.

About a year after Ponce returned to the New World,

he heard that King Ferdinand had died and his sixteen-year-old grandson, Charles I, would be the new Spanish king. Ponce realized he would have to defend his titles and privileges with the new king. Fortunately, Ponce remained in favor with Charles I and was requested to go on with his work in the islands. Ponce's wife, Leonor, also died at this time, so he had to get his own family affairs in order.

Between 1519 and 1521, the settlers at Caparra had moved to a little island in the harbor, and the town was renamed San Juan. Ponce's settlement on Puerto Rico was thriving. Now it was finally time to return to La Florida and make a permanent settlement. He had heard of at least two other explorers who had visited "his" Florida, but there had been, as yet, no permanent settlement. He would need to act fast to complete his mission. In February of 1521, Ponce was ready to sail again.

Much had happened since his first voyage to La Florida in 1513. Ponce had been busy in Spain or fighting the Caribs while other explorers were finding out more about this New World. By 1521 it was known that Florida was not an island. It was attached to a huge continent. Other explorers were now busy trying to find paths through that continent. One explorer, Vasco Nunez de Balboa, crossed a narrow part of the continent

Routes of many explorers around and across Florida (Courtesy of the State Archives of Florida)

and discovered yet another ocean. Balboa named it the Southern Sea. (We now know it as the Pacific Ocean.) Mexico had been discovered, and Hernan Cortes, with a large force of 350 men, was on his way to defeating the native Aztec tribe living there. Europe was just bursting with the latest exciting news from the explorers.

There is little written about Ponce's second voyage to Florida. He may have taken two ships and over a hundred men. He had some soldiers, priests, and skilled workers. They also had about fifty horses, to be used for riding as well as for use on the farms. They had seeds for new gardens and farming implements. Ponce must have been feeling certain that his settlement would be a success since he had his nephew, Hernan Ponce de Leon, along on the trip.

Eight years before, on his first landing on the Gulf side of Florida, Ponce had had a bad experience with the Calusa Indians. This time he may have headed just north of Charlotte Harbor. Arriving at southwest Florida in March of 1521, the ships looked for a suitable, and more peaceful, port. They searched for a safe harbor with easy access to open water. The lovely islands of Sanibel and Captiva were probably passed by in favor of having his permanent settlement on the mainland. He knew that fertile soil was important for their new farms. He might have been thinking of creating a town like Salvaleon.

They landed and started to build homes, but this settlement would not be permanent. It would last only about four months. The Calusa Indians attacked again and again. One final battle chased the Spaniards from their shores. Both sides fought furiously, but even with their metal weapons, the Spaniards were no match for so many Calusa. Many died in the repeated attacks, and Juan Ponce de Leon was badly injured.

Ponce was hit by an arrow in his thigh. His men carried him and other wounded men back to the ships. The ships quickly withdrew from port while arrows flew

View of the inlets and river at Charlotte Harbor (Courtesy of the State Archives of Florida)

through the air around them.

They sailed for Cuba as quickly as possible. Cuba had Spanish settlers and they hoped a Spanish doctor would be able to save Ponce. Some of the men died before they made it to port, including Ponce's nephew, Hernan.

Doctors in Cuba did their best, but Juan Ponce de Leon died from his wounds. Ponce was 47 years old. He was buried there and later his remains were taken to Puerto Rico. You can still see his tomb at the Catedral de San Juan Bautista (Cathedral of St. John the Baptist) in the city of San Juan.

Chapter 9

Remembering Juan Ponce de Leon

Columbus' first voyage to the New World was the beginning of a new excitement in the European countries. People wanted to know everything about the new lands that had been found. Many wanted to be first to discover another new island or mountain or sea. Not even fierce Indian raids could stop the enthusiasm. Even after the raids by the Calusa, with men dying around them, some of Ponce's crew may have sailed from Florida to join Cortes and the fighting in Mexico.

Juan Ponce de Leon was a part of that excitement. He is an important figure in our history because he made his own special discoveries.

One after the other, adventurers revealed secrets

about a whole new continent. Christopher Columbus crossed the ocean in 1492 and returned to tell about it. The following year, Ponce de Leon joined the adventurers. Three years later, explorers were already looking for a way through the land to again look for China and Japan!

By 1502, just ten years later, Amerigo Vespucci had investigated the east coast of the New World. The "Americas" were named for him. By 1519, Ferdinand Magellan had renamed Balboa's "Southern Sea" to be the Pacific Ocean. Magellan's ships then continued on and sailed completely around the world!

By 1521, many discoveries had been made, and permanent settlements had followed. Florida still awaited permanent settlement, but it would be almost fifty years before that would be accomplished. In the meantime, Hernando de Soto and his men went inland in Florida, finding many clear rivers, streams, and bubbling springs. The year 1559 saw perhaps two settlements by Spaniards in the Pensacola area of Florida's Panhandle, but they, too, did not last.

In 1564, a Frenchman, Jean Ribault, set up a colony near where Jacksonville, Florida, is today. The Spaniards did not want France to control Florida, so Pedro Menendez de Aviles was sent to drive the French out. In 1565, Menendez started the first permanent settlement in Florida, St. Augustine.

A drawing of Pedro Menendez de Aviles (Courtesy of the State Archives of
Florida)

At that time, La Florida was the name given to the whole Atlantic side of North America, from today's state of Florida up to southern Canada, stretching west across to the Mississippi River. Over the years that followed, French, English, and other explorers made their own settlements and reduced the size of La Florida.

By the 1700s, Florida was just today's state plus land to the west that extended to the Mississippi River. For a while the territory was divided by the Apalachicola River into East and West Florida, and for twenty years Florida was claimed by England. By 1817 Florida became a territory of the new United States.

Puerto Rico also changed over the years. After the discovery by Columbus and the government under Juan Ponce de Leon, it remained under Spanish rule until the early 1800s. The Puerto Rican people then sought independence from Spain and did get some control over their government. Today Puerto Rico is a self-governing territory of the United States of America. It is officially known as a commonwealth. Hispaniola is now the independent countries of the Dominican Republic and Haiti.

Juan Ponce de Leon's life is celebrated in the Caribbean islands and in Florida. He is remembered as a brave explorer, but he was also a farmer and a family

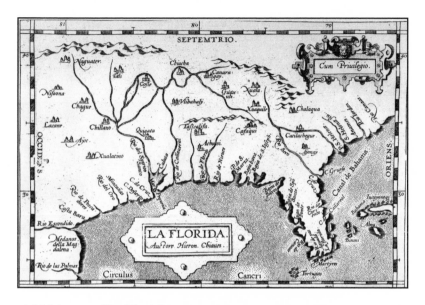

A 1584 map of La Florida (Courtesy of the State Archives of Florida)

man. Many of the other adventurers left their homes and families to go off to discover new lands. Ponce de Leon married Leonor and raised a family on Hispaniola and Puerto Rico. If Diego Columbus had not made life hard for him in Puerto Rico, he may never have found Florida.

Many explorers at that time were called "conquistadors." They would find a new land and take gold or whatever they wanted from it. Ponce de Leon realized the need to learn from the natives about their crops. He learned how to plant a good, productive garden in a new world. He learned how to rule as peaceably as possible. He will be remembered as being an explorer who made two very important discoveries. He was the first European we know of to find and attempt to settle the land we now call Florida. And he was the first we know of to sail into the Gulf Stream. The story of his life is a vital and important part of the history of our world.

Afterword

There is a legend about Ponce de Leon that should be a part of his story. For years people have thought there might be a "Fountain of Youth." This would be a spring of water that you could bathe in or drink and then you would become young again. The legend is as old as the Bible, or perhaps even older.

Some say that Ponce was searching for that fountain on his voyages. Perhaps he had been asked by King Ferdinand, who was an older man, to try to find that wonderful fountain. We do not know for sure that was one of the reasons for Ponce's explorations. But who knows?

If Ponce had been searching for a Fountain of Youth, he certainly was looking in the right place. Visitors come from far and wide, even today, to experience the beauty of Florida's springs and the peace there. One such spring is named after Ponce de Leon: DeLeon Springs, in central Florida.

Other places as well were named after this Spanish explorer. One place where he might actually have landed in 1513 on his first voyage to Florida is called Ponce Inlet. The tall lighthouse there is called Ponce de Leon Lighthouse. One of St. Augustine's main streets is called Ponce de Leon Boulevard. A main street in San Juan, Puerto Rico, is also named for him.

Juan Ponce de Leon will be remembered as the Spanish explorer who gave Florida, and possibly Puerto Rico, their names. He was the first Spanish-appointed governor of Spanish-claimed Florida. He was also the first Spanish-appointed governer of Puerto Rico. He braved the unknown and will be remembered for his discoveries.

Statue of Juan Ponce de Leon in St. Augustine today *(Courtesy of the State Archives of Florida)*

To See and Do

In Florida

DeLeon Springs

A town in central Florida near DeLand is named DeLeon Springs. DeLeon Springs State Park is at 601 Ponce DeLeon Boulevard in DeLeon Springs. It is a lovely place to visit, with picnic areas and a bubbling spring. Get ready for cold water if you want to swim there. The water stays a constant 72 degrees all year. www. FloridaStateParks.org

Jacksonville

Fort Caroline National Memorial
The Ribault Monument is atop St. Johns Bluff overlooking

the St. Johns River. Visitors will also see some of natural Florida by walking the trails of the 46,000-acre Timucuan preserve there. It is old Florida at its finest, preserved by the National Parks Service. www.nps.gov

Ponce de Leon Inlet
This inlet from the Atlantic Ocean is just north of New Smyrna Beach. There is also a town there called Ponce Inlet. You can visit the Ponce de Leon Inlet Lighthouse and Museum at 4931 South Peninsula Drive, Ponce Inlet. You will see the lighthouse and buildings in which the lighthouse keeper and his family might have lived. This tower is the tallest lighthouse in Florida, and one of the tallest in America. www.Ponceinlet.org

St. Augustine
Fountain of Youth Archaeological Park
You can visit this 15-acre waterfront historical attraction, with a planetarium, native Timucuan village, and interesting facts about Juan Ponce de Leon, at 11 Magnolia Avenue in St. Augustine. www. FountainOfYouthFlorida.com

St. Augustine Lighthouse and Museum
At 81 Lighthouse Avenue in St. Augustine, visitors

can see the 165-foot-tall lighthouse and a lighthouse keeper's house. The museum is dedicated to the preservation of the past and to keeping alive the story of the nation's oldest port. There are educational tours. You can learn about shipwrecks off Florida's coast. www. StAugustineLighthouse.com

There are many historical museums up and down the coasts of Florida which tell of the early Indians and the early history of each area.

In Puerto Rico

San Juan Cathedral

Also called Catedral de San Juan Bautista (Cathedral of St. John the Baptist), this beautiful Gothic structure is on Cristo Street in old San Juan. It is one of the city's oldest buildings, originally built with wooden walls and a thatch roof. Ponce de Leon's remains are in a marble tomb at the church. www.catedralsanjuan.com

Glossary

administrator – one who rules over others

ancient – very old

Boriquen – an old name for Puerto Rico

Caribs – a tribe of Indians who lived in the Caribbean

cassava – a shrub, also called yucca, and food made from the root of that shrub

commonwealth – a group of states or nations

East Indies – the many islands of Southeast Asia, including the nation of India

exotic – far from the usual; very different and beautiful

gallant – brave, grand

Hispaniola – a Caribbean island, now Haiti on the west
end and the Dominican Republic on the east

isolated – alone

legend – a popular story thought to be historical

log book – a notebook used by sailors to write daily
events

nativity – a place of birth

peninsula – land with water around it on 3 sides

primary – first in rank of importance; earliest

uncharted – a place that has not yet been mapped

viceroy – a title given by a king to someone, allowing
him to rule a land

yucca – *see* cassava

Selected Bibliography

Fuson, Robert H. *Juan Ponce de Leon and the Spanish Discovery of Puerto Rico and Florida.* Blacksburg, VA: McDonald & Woodward Publishing Company, 2000.

Otfinoski, Steven. *Juan Ponce de Leon: Discoverer of Florida.* (Great Explorations Series). Tarrytown, NY: Benchmark Books, 2005.

Acknowledgments

Sincere thanks to the following people who have read over this manuscript: Dr. Samuel Turner, Director of Archaeology, Lighthouse Archaeological Maritime Program (LAMP), St. Augustine Lighthouse & Museum, St. Augustine; Amy Cervantes, K-5 social studies specialist, Volusia County Schools; Joan Westhrin, head librarian, and Dave Miner, librarian, at the Southeast Volusia Historical Society Museum in New Smyrna Beach, Florida; Barbara Shew, retired librarian from Ithaca (N.Y.) High School, and Randall Shew, journalist and retired administrator at Cornell University; my creative husband, Bob Sammons; and Phyllis Lewis, a true friend for years. I thank them all for their expertise. Any errors that may have crept in I must claim as my own.

Index

Numbers in *italics* indicate illustrations.

Here are some other books from Pineapple Press on related topics. For a complete catalog, visit our website at www.pineapplepress.com. Or write to Pineapple Press, P.O. Box 3889, Sarasota, Florida 34230-3889, or call (800) 746-3275.

Also by Sandra Wallus Sammons

Marjory Stoneman Douglas and the Florida Everglades. Read about the "grandmother of the Everglades," from her childhood up north to her long and inspiring life in south Florida. She won the Presidential Medal of Freedom for her work. Ages 9–12.

Marjorie Kinnan Rawlings and the Florida Crackers. Marjorie Kinnan Rawlings always loved to write. When she moved to Cross Creek in Florida, she began to write stories about the Crackers she met. *The Yearling,* about a boy and his pet deer, won a Pulitzer Prize for fiction. Ages 9–12.

The Two Henrys: Henry Plant and Henry Flagler and Their Railroads. Henry Plant and Henry Flagler changed the landscape of Florida in the late 1800s and early 1900s. This dual biography is the story of railroads and the men whose innovation and money built them. Flagler opened up the east coast of Florida with his railroads and hotels, and Plant did the same on the west coast. Ages 12 and up.

Henry Flagler, Builder of Florida. Henry Morrison Flagler was already a millionaire when he first visited Florida in 1878. He came back and built railroads along the east coast of the state so others could more easily travel there. Then he built grand hotels so those travelers had a place to stay. By 1912 he had built a railroad all the way to Key West. Determined and practical, Flagler met all the great challenges he set for himself. Ages 9–12.

Other Young Reader Titles

The Treasure of Amelia Island by M.C. Finotti. Mary Kingsley, the youngest child of former slave Ana Jai Kingsley, recounts the life-changing events of December 1813. Her family lives in La Florida, a Spanish territory under siege by Patriots who see no place for freed people of color in a new Florida. Against these mighty events, Mary decides to search for a legendary pirate treasure with her brothers. Ages 8–12; fiction.

Escape to the Everglades by Edwina Raffa and Annelle Rigsby. Based on historical fact, this young adult novel tells the story of Will Cypress, a half-Seminole boy living among his mother's people during the Second Seminole War. He meets Chief Osceola and travels with him to St. Augustine. Ages 9–14; fiction.

Kidnapped in Key West by Edwina Raffa and Annelle Rigsby. Twelve-year-old Eddie Malone is living in the Florida Keys in 1912 when suddenly his world is turned upside down. His father, a worker on Henry Flagler's Over-Sea Railroad, is thrown into jail for stealing the railroad payroll. Eddie is determined to prove his father's innocence. But then the real thieves kidnap Eddie. Can he escape? Will he ever get home? Will he be able to prove Pa's innocence? Ages 8–12; fiction.